# NOWADAYS HRM ROLE IN ORGANIZATION

JOHN LOK

ISBN 979-888591024-8

# Contents

*Preface* v

*Prologue* vii

1. Traditional Human Resource Management Strategy Changes 1

2. Nowadays Hrm Reward Management Strategy 14

3. Human Resource Role Nowadays Changes 35

# Preface

What are the HRM strategy difference between past tradtional HRM and nowadays HRM ?Why human resource strategy can bring organizational benefits. How nowadays reward strategy can bring what kinds of benefits to organizations.

Reward management is nowadays considered as an important topic in order to achieve the goals of a company. Employees are considered as the main factor which plays an important role in the organization. The success of each and every organization is its dedicated employee's .Current world is filled with changes and competition. In order to survive in the current situation companies should be having employees who are loyal and expert in their own field. New technologies are developed constantly and the companies are eagerly trying to catch up those talented employees with right expertise in their own areas. So, fair award management can attract talented employees to choose the organization to work. When the organization has good reward management, then it will bring good organizational development, good learning and training ,
good performance management, good sourcing and staff, good employee engagement.

In my this book, I shall explain how and why nowadays good reward management will bring all above these any one of human resource related issues to let readers to make accurate and reasonable analysis. I will explain how any why effective department communication, excellent technological input, effective human resource developement training, good employee motivation strategy and effective performance measurement strategy can influence any organization's overall performance to be more effective. I shall indicate the reasons to explain why above any one of these factors have indirect relationship to influence the organization's overall performance effectiveness. Readers can learn how and why HRM strategy changes can influence organization's overall performance to achieve more effectiveness to compare traditional HR strategy.

# Prologue

Table of content

Chapter 1
Traditional Human resource management strategy changes p.4-26
Chapter 2
Nowadays HRM Reward management strategy p.27-44
Chapter 3

Human resource role nowadays changes p.45-66

CHAPTER ONE

# Traditional Human resource management strategy changes

Nowadays, large organizations are expanding and employees and customers number is also increasing. It is difference to general past traditional business organizations, they are small size and less employees number. So, nowadays any large organizations' human resource department management methods or strategies are very different to past traditional small size organizations. What are their differences in HR management strategies aspect. I shall give some
opinions to explain whether what are their HR department operation differences as below:

Why Strategic Human Resource Management (SHRM) is so important? Nowadays, Strategic Human Resource Management becomes very important for the organizations in the business world environment. The purpose of this assignment is about what the Strategic Human Resource Management (SHRM) is and why SHRM is so important? How is human resource management (HRM) strategic to a firm's viability and how it might help to lay a basis for sustained competitive advantage? And what are the strategies for the managers to pursue their goals for labor productivity and organizational flexibility
in socially acceptable ways.

HRM has existed in one form or another since the beginning of time. Certain HR functions, even though informal in nature, were performed whenever people came together for a common purpose. During this century, the processes of managing people have become more formalized and specialized.However, due to nowadays organizations are increasing

employees number and customers number, so it can influence HR department needs to change their management strategy to adapt marketing need. It means that nowadays and past traditional HR department tasks and function and responsibility must
have much change to compare before.

Example of a firm's human resources to gain competitive advantage may include as below:

Strategic human resource management (SHRM) takes the ideas one step further by emphasizing the need for HR plans and strategies to be
formulated within the context of overall organizational strategies and objectives, and to be responsive to the changing nature of the organization's external 'environment' (i.e. its competitors, the national and international arenas). A strong implication of SHRM theory is that HR plans and strategies should be developed on a long-term basis, taking into account likely changes in the society, industrial relations systems, economic conditions, legislation, global and technological issues, as well as new directions in business operations.

People is the source of competitive edge, there are different ways of competing are significant for managing human resources because they help determine needed employee behaviors. That is, for competitive strategies to be successfully implemented, employees have to behave in certain ways. And for employees to behave in certain ways, human resource practices need to be put in place that help ensure that those behaviors are explained, are possible, and are rewarded.

Nordstrom exists in the highly competitive retailing industry. This industry is usually characterized as having relatively low skill requirements and high turnover for sales clerks. Nordstrom has attempted to focus on individual salespersons as the key to its competitive advantage. It invests in attracting and retaining young, college-educated sales clerks who desire a career in retailing. It provides a highly incentive based compensation system that allows Nordstron's salespersons to make as much as twice the industry average in pay. The Nordstrom culture encourages sales clerks to make heroic dfforts to attend to customers' needs, even to the point of changing a customer's tyre in the parking lot . the recruiting process, compensation practices, and culture at Nordstron have helped the organization tomaintain the
highest sales per square foot of any retailer in the nation. (Source: Black, J. A., & Boal, K. B. (1994). Traits, Configurations and paths to sustainable

competitive advantage.)

(1) Past traditional HRM strategy

Traditional HRM strategy means that industrial and Salaried Model of Traditional Human Resource Management. The industrial model of the human resource management traditional approach, applicable to blue-collared factory workers, is a controlled work atmosphere marked by narrow, rigid job definitions and detailed workplace rules and procedures. Workers have much autonomy and deviating from the written policy and procedure attract disciplinary action, with discretion remaining an exclusive prerogative of management. The trade union dominates collective bargaining settlements define pay scales, and seniority decides promotion opportunities.

The salaried model of the human resource management traditional approach, applicable to white-collar jobs have less rigid terms of

employment and broadly defined job descriptions, but the basic concept of a tightly defined work structure in terms of written job responsibilities and sticking to the brief,

with only top managers considered competent to take major decisions remains. Merit, as determined by the performance appraisal procedure and educational qualifications, ranks paramount in deciding promotions and pay fixation.The major characteristics of the human resource management traditional approach common to both the industrial model and salaried model

focus on functional activities and process orientation, control activities, and reconciliation between management and workforce.

Focus on Functional Activities and Process Orientation

Human resource management traditional approaches focus on functional activities such as human resource planning, job analysis, recruitment and selection, maintaining employee relations, performance appraisals, compensation management, and training and development. The traditional approach toward human resource management also focuses on establishing policies, procedures, contracts and guidelines, and attempts to drive employee performance and achieve organizational goals by making employees adhere to such carefully crafted documents.For instance, the recruitment and selection activity strictly follows laid down norms such as undertaking a job analysis first, advertising the vacancy based on the job specifications and job requirements, collecting resumes, conducting written tests, interviews and any other selection method, as well as creating a rank list based on the published selection criteria. Such clear rules and written procedures extend to all gamuts of human resource activities.

It usually remains standardized and inflexible, and considers the fulfillment of corporate strategic goals only marginally. It does, however, remain resilient to
incorporate trends such as Total Quality Management. The focus on functional activity and process orientation leads to the establishment of an institutionalized workforce management
effort with fixed grades and restrictive movement from one grade to another.

(2) What are the four stages of HRM department change from traditional to nowadays ?

IN any organizations, traditional HRM departments had been changed to nowadays department from traditional model, since many small or middle size organizations are demanded to expand to large ,even international organizations model. However, they must encounter these four stages to experience their organizational changes as well as how they influence HRM departments are also needed to be changed absolutely. I shall explain the four stages as below:

The first stage means Industrial Era HR stage, the $20^{th}$ century witnessed severe labor unrest due to the employment-at-will doctrine and yellow-dog contracts that allowed employers to fire employees at will. These rules also restricted employees from participating in union activities. Because of frequent strikes and lack of manpower, companies instituted personnel departments to perform administrative activities related to employees. This was the time labor unions became prevalent, and the personnel department was used to resolve wage-related issues and other differences between the union and management. The personnel manager was responsible for employee attendance, labor-dispute management and general compliances of employee health and safety requirements. The recruitment section of the personnel
department dealt mainly with selecting labor employees, along with a few salaried professionals.

The second stage means Post FLSA HR stage, the Fair Labor Standards Act of 1938 was instituted around the time of the great depression. The FLSA mandated minimum wages, which brought cheer to the working population along with other laws that safeguard employee interests.

Organizations set up management teams that handled various facets of business. As such, the personnel department's role evolved to primarily statutory compliance and employee health and safety concerns. At this time, training and development took precedence in businesses, and the human resource department was created to address the need. Key HR functions, therefore, included performance and succession management, along with training and development. Over time, the roles between HR and the personnel department blurred.

The third stage means 21st Century HR stage, changes in the economic conditions of the 21st century brought about the need for HR to take on additional responsibilities. HR staff, therefore, began actively participating in business decision-making. Often sharing a seat at the management table, they help determine when to downsize, outsource, retrain and recruit suitable talent. HR staff also participate in managing the cost of employee benefits such as insurance and pension and in handling other issues and activities such as creating and documenting policy, assisting with employee-related litigation and ensuring compliance with employment laws such as the Employee Retirement Income Security Act. Helping to determine the companies' overall direction, HR departments focus on building organizational capabilities using employee management and development strategies that align with organizational goals.

The final stage means Information Age HR stage, the invention of new technologies and improvements on old ones has introduced a way for businesses to work across international borders. Thus, information technologies and globalization has changed business processes and opened up new avenues and challenges for human resources. While the costs are reduced and manpower abundant, human resources areas experienced unforeseen challenges. Some of these challenges include difficulties in managing employees dispersed across the globe, adjusting to new cultures and allocating resources in a timely manner. Here, new options such as simulated training and resource management software help to bridge gaps. HR departments changed again to adapt to the information age and stay above the manpower challenges.

Hence, any nowadays organizations when they expand to the large size and employees and customers number is also influenced to increase. Then, their HR departments also need to follow their organizational needs change to influence whole organization HR department changes in the same time.

What is the nowadays HRM role after traditional HRM role is changed?

There are several factors in the changing function of HR in today's workforce, including modernized duties at companies, the use of technology in human resources and the responsibility of HR to help establish and maintain workplace culture. Throughout many industries, the role of HR has traditionally been considered one of policy development and paperwork, from developing employee handbooks, collecting time cards and drawing up contracts for new employees to managing employee benefits and handling worker complaints. Many industries have undergone tremendous change over the last several years due to evolving technology, new employment regulations and younger, more diverse workers.The role of HR departments has been particularly impacted by the growing availability of technology and self-serve digital tools, experts say.

Technology is making many of the traditional tasks of HR departments simpler and less time-consuming. Online human resource management tools now allow employees to do all but the most complex tasks themselves, he said, from signing up for and managing insurance to tracking their work hours and progress toward professional goals.Until the widespread use of HR technologies in the past decade, it was rare to see a HR department engaged in much more than daily transactional functions ... This shift towards self-service has allowed HR to put more resources into specialized functions such as benefits administration, leave management, employee relations and more," Sinclair said. "This focus on specialized functions has helped to change HR from a simple reactionary service to a team of experts who can be consulted by top management and front line employees alike.

As new companies form and grow, and new regulations and employment laws are passed, educated and experienced human resources managers will be in high demand across a wide range of industries to help ensure organizations follow the new guidelines and respond to changing employee needs. Still, as the human resource profession changes, competition for these jobs will also be high. If you're considering a career in human resources, it's important to understand how industry changes are impacting not only job prospects, but sought-after training and skills.With the influx of HR technologies, the field is becoming more specialized. Many new HR jobs added in the coming years, HRM will require more specialization and training from human

resource workers and job seekers. HR professionals will be required to become experts in one or two specific areas in order to adequately address these (industry) changes.This will definitely impact how HR professionals are trained now and in the future. No longer can folks just 'fall' into HR with no experience or background. The complexity of the profession in all areas requires a deeper understanding of the human resource function.

(3) Organizational development influences HRM strategy need changes

· Why do organizations need develop?

Organizational development (OD) is defined by theorists and practitioners in different ways. Essentially, it is a planned, organization-wide effort to increase an organization's effectiveness and/or to enable an organization to achieve its strategic goals. Before working on organizational development activities, an essential first step is to map the organizational context in which the changes , you are hoping what will occur. It means to understand function what affect your work, which approach you may be bringing to the activities and being able to determine an organization's readiness to work with you and develop for themselves the required innovations.

Many OD projects focus on providing the more visible material resources, building skills, improving organizational structures and systems. Moreover, culture values have an impact on several elements of as including: the way change occurs, perception about whether change is needed, perception about leadership and ownership , perception about risk and uncertainty, perception about relationship and partnership and perception of what success looks like. It is described internal changes as relating to organizational structures, processes and human resource requirement, whereas external changes involves government legislation, competitor movements and customer demand.

In general, organizational development aims to expect to raise awareness, e.g. improved understanding, attitude, confidence or motivation , enhanced knowledge and skills, e.g. increasing ability to act through teamwork, e.g. strengthened ability to act through improved with a group a people tied by a common task. This may involve for example, among them members, a stronger agreement or improved, communication, coordination, contribution by the team members to the common task, enhanced networks, e.g. improved processes for stronger incentives for participation in the network or increased traffic or communication among network members; increased implementation know -how , e.g. discovery and innovation with learning by doing formulation or implementation of policies, strategies, plans for UD aims in possible.

Why do organizations need to changed? Our business would is fasting to increase technology new methods of production and new taste of customers and new market trends as well as new strategies for best control of the organizations and motivation of employees like to accept to use new products in popular nowadays. Hence, managers need to concern how to decide about the change management in the organizations, because business activities now are globalize, and every organization needs to attract loyal customers , trained the employees, introduce and adapt new methods of production and best control the activities of the organization.

How will change organization in the good condition? The question arises in present scenario. Organizational change or change management aims to raise ability of the management benefits and support from change with reduced inefficiencies and ineffectiveness from the side of employees and encourage appreciate acceptance and support. The process of changing the activities of the organization as well as the implementation of the procedures and technologies to achieve the design objective. If the organization usually needs to change management includes different aspects, such as control change, adaptation change and effecting change.

Consequently, organizational change simply means to change the activities of the organization, it concerns change the culture of the organization, technology, business process, change of employees, rules and procedures, recruitment and selection, design of jobs, methods of appraisal , human resource , technology, physical environment of the organization, methods of training and development, job skill, and knowledge etc.

However, when the organization decides to implement change. Some employees should feel not adapt the change easily. They will quickly respond by complaints, engaging in work slowdown, threating to go on strike etc. How to overcome change management implementation successfully. The organizations need to implement change fairly , selection people who accept change, education and communication

However, organization development also plays an important role in the change management. It can be defined as a collection planned change, built a humanistic values and benefits and welfare needs, that need to improve the organizational effectiveness and employees work performance and well-being.

· Why does General Motor organization need change management?

For General Motor (GM) change management case example, GM taking swift cost cutting action (2008) showed GM established in 1908s, till 1920s it was becoming the world largest motor manufacturing company, it could produce new style and design car every year. These were different brand cars which were producing by the company that time, and this every there were no other competitors to compete in the company different cars. But, the Japan automakers the company, GM felt threatened, specially Toyota Japan. Hence, GM needed to again get his position in market by restructuring and making change in the company. Now the GM company is again operating business in core brands in America, such as GMC.

GM taking swift cost cutting action ( 2008) also indicated that however, the change to GM was the high wages cost to employees as the company was paying US$74 per hour as compared to Toyota US$44 per hour, because GM was an agreement with trade union and GM run the plant with minimum 80% capacity whether it was needed or not.

Hence, what types of changes are decided to bring or make change to GM. In fact GM decided to bring changes on some areas of the motor business. These were included, structural change, cost change, process change and cultural change. The steps which as taken to change by the GM is about cost cutting, it has reduced cost of some brands to maintain the profit level. Similarly , GM also cut pay of employees which was the major problem. The GM also changed the culture of the company. GM removed it automate producing board and automate strategy up to 8 men board. It can changed the culture to improve the efficiency of the employees and such change is to speed up the day to day decision making.

But, GM also encounters problems to change process. Such as problems in cultural change, the cultural plan was based top down approach, which ignored totally the involvement of the employees as compared to other companies, some suggested that it has not down up approach in which employees feel satisfaction. So this regard , it empowered the employees by introducing in tailoring the down top approach. Rather then telling to employees what they do, due to its employees hope have change to discuss with top management to express their opinions. Moreover, the other problem with cost cutting from the agreement of trade union, as it was an agreement with not lowering the pay of the employees and maintain the capacity level

·

Driving change at GM (2005) indicated that better result of cost cutting of GM seems from its employment figure of 98 to 2009. It was reduced from 226,000 to 101,000 workers and now the GM is concentrating on sale rather than to further cut off and also GM is deciding to reduce the worker force of the factory from 60,000 to 40,000. It certainly leads to cost saving to GM. Another better result of cultural change to GM, employees now becoming aware about the responsibility, as well as GM as empowered the employed to give better productivity. Hence, GM can success to solve change management problems to bring profit and win its competitors in motor sale market in global successfully.

· Culture can influence organization development

Culture is not the way we do things around here. Culture is which we cooperate and the through we view the organization. If we view an organization as a system of interacting and interrelated part, culture defines , creates and supports that system.

· IBM computer organizational culture influences whether it's computers will be out dated feeling to computer consumers. For IBM computer example, IBM had brought to change a culture means changing our fundamental view of how the world works. However, IBM ran into serious financial difficulties in the late 1980 and early 1990s in large part because it was unwilling to change the ways in which it was approaching the computer market, even though the market was rapidly changing around it to break with tradition.

How is culture created to IBM? Stephen, R.B(2011) indicated IBM founder , or the influential leader, had reinforced the values of culture. When he worked for IBM many years ago, he discovered the IBM leader was one considerable person to his employees. Such as one case, how when an IBM employee was badly injured and his family killed in a car accident, the leader Tom Watson was there at the hospital when the man woke up, promising to cover the medical bills and do whatever he could. Hence, he can let IBM employees feel that IBM was seem to their home family.

Hence, what makes a successful culture to IBM ? Stephen, R.B(2011) also showed that a culture is successful if it is in harmony with its environment and unsuccessful if it it unable to function in its environment. The environment is the world in which the culture operates. So, when environment changes faster than cultures. When the environment changes, the mechanisms of the culture may no longer be valid. Such as the advent of the PC changed the business environment for IBM, and the company found it difficult indeed to adjust. Today, with the accelerating shift from desktop computers to mobile devices and the Internet, Microsoft is still. In 1992, IBM had a loss for the first time, closed down numerous divisions. However, IBM's culture contained a very strong ethic of " analyze the problem, determine the solution, and execute the solution even, if it 's unpleasant." IBM realized that it needed a fresh perspective, so it brought in Lou Gerstner, the first non-IBM to become CEO. As Ed Schein points out, Gerstner came from a very similar marketing background to IBM's founder, Tom Watson, Sr. Gerstner didn't so much change IBM's culture as revitalize an aspect of it that had become dormant. Over the year, IBM's engineering culture had become dominant, and the marketing culture had benefit to become into the background.

· IKEA organizational culture influences whether it's China furniture market in success?

Why does IKEA management cultural diversity needs to regard its staffs in China challenge? Multinational company, such as IKEA furniture company aims to increase profitability and it also needs to seek to for solutions to problems related with the saturation of existing markets, it needs to make an effort to expand operations to overseas market, such as China. However, it will face cultural difference challenge to be needed to deal if it want to enter China furniture sale market successfully.

Kumar, S. (2005) indicated IKEA is the world's largest furniture retailer since the early 1990s. It offers a wide range of well- designed, functional home furniture products at low prices as many people as possible will be able to afford them. However, IKEA planned to enter China market, but it will face the cultural difference challenge between China and itself Swedish regional cultural of their staff communication and co-operational relationship.

In deed, the "IKEA" facilities its successfully international expansions , it needs to combination vision, characteristic leadership and business principle between China and Swedish culture effectively. IKEA opened its first store in China in 1998. Although, the company has succeeded with their global strategy in the past in most of the markets, it has entered , it quickly learnt the success in the Chinese market required a different strategy in the areas of marketing and HR ( Kumar, 2005, p.2).

What are the cultural difference to influence IKEA's success to develop furniture sale in China market? The standardized strategy which is adopted by IKEA could lead to some disadvantages because Swedish managers are needed to send to other branches in other countries in other to ensure the IKEA way is implemented in the local areas. Thus, it brings the conflict between the Swedish management and local employees could occur due to the cultural differences. Especially, in the country like China where the traditional cultures and value are different to such as Swedish culture. So, Chinese employees will have their mind for long a working culture differs from the Swedish way that IKEA wants to influence to their employees, problems were unavailable.

When IKEA were keen to increase revenue in Asian markets like China, they faced the challenge to mange their staffs from the conflicts and the diversity of Chinese cultures, such as how to train people within IKEA perform in a standardized format to keep its essential value, and how to avoid the misunderstanding when improve employee performance and understanding the importance of cross cultural management between Sweden and China. So, IKEA managers definitely have responsibilities to spend time, energy and effort to understand the differences of national corporate and functional cultures before starting an arranging the strategic plans in China furniture sale market.

The another cultural difference challenge concerns China and Sweden both countries have problems on law, price competition, information, language, delivery, foreign currency, time differences and cultural differences etc. different aspects. Thus, such as this IKEA Sweden furniture international company plans to enter China furniture sale market. It will have great barriers are caused by cultural differences, such as difficulty of communication, higher potential transaction costs, different objectives and means of cooperation and operating methods.

These problems have led to the failure to IKEA furniture to enter China furniture sale market in possible. Therefore, IKEA needs to concern questions how to do business in China and understand China's culture and how to do business with Chinese people. It is possible that Chinese labors dissatisfy IKEA's provided cheap labor as well as the strong serious organizational bureaucracy system, high job duty demand is needed to satisfy customer's behavior in China. Hence, IKEA's culture difference challenge to China furniture sale market , it has relationship to human resource management and reward challenge.

How nowadays HRM changes to develop?

Human Resource Development is the framework for helping employees develops their personal and organizational skills, knowledge, and abilities. Organizations have many opportunities for human resources or employee development, both within and outside of the workplace. By the end of this paper i will be able to devise a human resource plan for a work area, to meet organizational objectives, identify and plan for individual development to meet organizational objectives and also initiate a personal development plan for an individual and evaluate progress. Healthy organizations believe in Human Resource Development and cover all of these bases.

The focus of all aspects of Human Resource Development is on developing the most superior workforce so that the organization and individual employees can accomplish their work goals in service to customers. We need to learn new skills and develop new abilities, to respond to these changes in our lives, our careers, and our organizations. We can deal with these constructively, using change for our competitive advantage and as opportunities for personal and organizational growth, or we can be overwhelmed by them. With all the downsizing, outsourcing and team building, responsibility and accountability are being downloaded to individuals. So everyone is now a manager. Everyone will need to acquire and/or increase their skills, knowledge and abilities to perform their jobs. By developing our knowledge and skills, our actions and standards, our motivation, incentives, attitudes and work environment we will be able to cope up with the ever changing work environment.

CHAPTER TWO

# Nowadays HRM Reward management strategy

What is reward management strategy? It may define that it can influence your organization's employee individual productive efficiency raising and/or service performance improvement,it can influence your organization's employee individual emotion and working attitude to be changed more positive to raise productive efficiency and/or service performance as well as
it can raise employee individual skill level in order to raise productive efficiency and/or service performance.

Why does organizations need reward management strategy that is concerned with the formulation and implementation of strategies and policies that aim to reward people fairly, equitably and consistently in accordance with their value to the organization ?Reward management consists of analyzing and controlling employee remuneration, compensation and all of
the other benefits for the employees. Reward management aims to create and efficiently operate a reward structure for an organization. Reward structure usually consists of pay policy and practices, salary and payroll administration, total reward, minimum wage, executive pay and team reward.

Reward is the generic term for the totality of financial and non-financial compensation or total remuneration paid to an employee in return for work or service rendered at work. Reward, which is sometimes been refer to as compensation or remuneration, is perhaps the most important contract term in every paid-employment.
Its impact on workers (or employee's) performance is in most instance

greatly misinterpreted. The understanding of this term is very important; this is because the incentive scheme given to an employee will influence the behavior and level of engagement to the organization. However, basic pay, it is a straightforward payment scheme which may not provide incentives to individual workers because they are not based on output or performance. This pay is often in relation to a given period like an hourly rate, weekly wage or annual salary. It's also an established rate for all workers in one category. Incentive for group, Plant/enterprise-based it is refer to as grain sharing within large group or the whole organization. This pay scheme is use in
organizations where the workforce can clearly see the results of their efforts.

Award can include two kinds. Intrinsic reward include- Achievement, feeling of accomplishment, recognition, job satisfaction, personal growth and status, job enlargement, job enrichment, team working, empowerment. Otherwise, extrinsic rewards also include formal-recognition; base wage or salary, incentive payments, fringe benefits, promotion, social relationship and work environment. This study will explain and define different type of pay and non-financial scheme use in today's organizations.

Reward Management is concerned with the formulation and implementation of strategies and policies that aim to reward people fairly, equitably and consistently in accordance with their value to the organization. Reward management forms the organization relationship. This if an HR manager is to succeed in successfully managing the employment relationship, he/she will have to do well in reward management, otherwise these will be an in balance in the employment relationship, such as strikes, lockouts. Objectives of Reward Management may include: Support the organization's strategy, recruit & retain, motivate employees, internal & external equity, strengthen psychological contract, financially sustainable, comply with legislation and efficiently administered.

Basic Types of Reward include

· Extrinsic rewards

– satisfy basic needs: survival, security

– Pay, conditions, treatment

· Intrinsic rewards

– satisfy higher needs: esteem, development

Rewards by Individual, Team, Organization

· Individual: base pay, incentives, benefits
– rewards attendance, performance, competence
· Team
– team bonus, rewards group cooperation
· Organization
– profit-sharing, shares, gain-sharing

In general , a profitable reward management system should have these characteristics: Simplicity must be easily understood by everyone in the organization. People must understand why they are getting, what they are getting from the employment relationship . Fairness and equitability, every component of the system must be justifiable and consistently applied. But reward management has related problems, such as strike, staff turnover, dissatisfaction etc. An effective participatory reward management system should be negotiated and agreed better management and employees.

What is the role of Nowadays Compensation and Reward in Organization?
Compensation and Reward system plays vital role in a business organization. Since, among four Ms, i.e. Men, Material, Machine and Money, Men has been most important factor, it is impossible to imagine a business process without Men. Land, Labor, Capital and Organization are four major factors of production.

Every factor contributes to the process of production/business. It expects return from the business process such as rent is the return expected by the Landlord. Similarly Capitalist expects interest and organizers i.e. Entrepreneur expects profits. The labor expects wages from the process. It is evident that other factors are in-human factors and as such labor plays vital role in bringing about the process of production/business in motion. The other factors being human, has expectations, emotions, ambitions and egos. Labor therefore expects to have fair share in the business/production process.

What are the advantages of Fair Compensation System?
Therefore a fair compensation system is a must for every business organization. The fair compensation system will help in the following:
· If an ideal compensation system is designed, it will have positive impact on the efficiency and results produced by workmen.

· Such system will encourage the normal worker to perform better and achieve the standards fixed.

· This system will encourage the process of job evaluation. It will also help in setting up an ideal job evaluation, which will have transparency, and the standards fixing would be more realistic and achievable.

· Such a system would be well defined and uniform. It will be apply to all the levels of the organization as a general system.

· The system would be simple and flexible so that every worker/recipient would be able to compute his own compensation receivable.

· Such system would be easy to implement, so that it would not penalize the workers for the reasons beyond their control and would not result in exploitation of workers.

· It will raise the morale, efficiency and cooperation among the workers. It, being just and fair would provide satisfaction to the workers.

· Such system would help management in complying with the various labor acts.

· Such system would also bring about amicable settlement of disputes between the workmen union and management.

· The system would embody itself the principle of equal work equal wages. Encouragement for those who perform better and opportunities for those who wish to excel.

Factors affect an organization's nowadays reward policy and strategy which include: affordability, it means what an organization can afford to pay the argument is that an organization can't borrow to reward employees, but should reward from the value created by the employees themselves. However, an organization has to afford to pay above legal minimums, legislation sets the minimum base pay ( minimum fixed pay rates), which becomes the starting point in calculating for all of an organization's policies. Workers committees/trade unions depend on the power of a union, pay levels are determined through collective bargaining. The most powerful ones will strike higher levels, external job value means the market value of the job, e.g. what is the market value or HR manager or clerical assistant? Internal job value means the value or perceived value of a job compared to other jobs which the organization will determine the reward that job, e.g. HR manager compared to finance manager. Value of the person means employees holding similar jobs can be paid differently depending on the value of the organization performance and the economy environment influence means ( labor supply/demand). Some authors explained a depressed economy increased the supply of labor, which reduced its price and have effect reward policy strategy.Thus, reward system strategy means a benefit plan management procedure and it needs to implement these steps in order to achieve its fair reward as below:

Step one, deciding objective to assess what the company wants to achieve through its benefit strategy and policy, and its ability to pay for the changes;

Step two, obtaining view points and input from employees to collect employees' view points through employee surveys, focus groups and individual interviews;

Step third, analyzing competitiveness to establish or determine the company's competitive position, though conducting a customized survey or collecting available market data from external providers;

Step fourth, designing the benefit package to determine the mix and scale of the benefit package, the allocation of benefit, the scope for flexibility and the cost of benefit provision;

Step fifth, consulting the senior management team and employees on the proposal to get input and buy in from senior management team to make amendments if necessary, collecting comments and effort the non-financial rewards as benefits; step sixth, planning the communication to inform everyone concerned what is happening, why it is happening and how it affects them,

The final step , evaluation to review the plan on a regular basis and obtain input from employees and management for evaluation purposes.

Strategy reward system pay for perform two elements: Financial reward includes base salary, pay incentives, employee benefits. Non-financial reward includes intrinsic rewards, centers in the work itself, praise, recognition , time off. Reward system is a key driver of-HR strategy, business strategy organization culture strategic reward system related to HR system. Such as skill-based pay to training, overtime pay rules to labor relations, sign-on bonus to employment, merit pay to performance management and merit pay to performance culture.

Thus one successful reward strategy system will have these characteristics. Performance and reward strategy, identify requirement and develop strategy, analyze data and performance and reward information on individuals or group and achieve colleges to aid decision making, work with managers to certain and develop reward requirements for key individuals within their area, review and analyze the organization strategy demographic profile and market activity against current reward activity to identify current reward activity to identify current and long term reward requirement to assess internal and external factors driving reward requirements against plan. Explain to employees how pay and reward fits and supports overall people processes and activities, such as performance management.

In conclusion, what is award's aim ? For the organisation, reward should aim at; recruiting the quantity and quality required, encourage suitable staff to be loyal and remain in the organisation, provide rewards for good performance and incentives for further improvement in performance, maintain appropriate differentials relative to values of different levels of job, the reward adopted by organisation should be flexible enough to accommodate changes in the market rate for different skills and should be cost effective. For individual employees the reward system should be fair and equitable in valuation of the worth in comparison with others. The third which is the union of employees, the system should ensure maximum benefits for members without undue prejudices to their future security by making their reward to pace with the cost of living and the prosperity of the organisation.

What kinds of benefits of reward strategy which can bring to organizations? Good employee benefits and services can help the organization by reducing potential employee discontent, satisfying their needs and discouraging labor unrest or raising labor turnover. Thus, with competitive benefit programs , an organization can be more effective in recruitment and employee retention, thus reducing labor turnover.

Employee benefits may include legally required payments, such as workers compensation, long service pay or retirement payment, sickness allowance and end of year payment, bonus as well as optional welfare plans, such as life insurance, medical/hospital /dental coverage to self and family' education allowance, housing allowance, quarters, subsidized loans, retirement, pension plan, meal allowance, travelling allowance, paid time off, pay sick leave, other special paid leave, five day week, paid annual leave and maternity leave.

Employee service mean the organizations can choose to provide various services ranging from work related to those satisfying personal or family needs, in order to encourage employees to work happily and stay with a particular organization. The service may include social functions or recreational activities, e.g. New Year dinner, annual ball, company picnics, free transportation service, food service or canteen ,purchase of used equipment no longer required by the company, credit unions, low-interest loans, legal services, child care and elder care services, free holiday apartment, air ticket allowance etc. employees' welfares.

Why do some organizations need to change reward management system?

Some HR professionals feel reward management can earn these benefits to organizations. In compensation and benefits reward management aspect, it is not possible to imagine an offer of employment that does not indicate a salary or wage and possibly other terms of compensation as well as description of the various benefits available with the employment. So, a candidate accepts or rejects the job offer, he/she will regard how a compensation package with a monetary of non-monetary value, such as a fair exchange for whose labor. So, the award management plan will include monetary reward and non-monetary reward both is better than monetary reward only. For example, piece rate pay is good for factory workers, commissions have long been a major part of the compensation of salespeople and merit pay and bonuses are well established methods of rewarding good performance for car salespeople. So, the variable or incentive pay is a good reward implementation plan for salespeople, insurance agents.

How to evaluate the base pay level is the more accurate? Leon, M. (2002) indicated that when a company needs to determine levels of base pay, the best companies have several objectives. The most important , in a global business environment characterized by strong demand for talented experienced employees is to be competitive. The determination of base pay level does not depend on only in one's own industry, but also in other

industries competing for the same talent. In fact, a firm's closes competition for human resources often is not its closet industrial competitor. In addition, the best companies are attractive to the levels of compensation appropriate to the different regions and countries where facilities are located or where workers originate. At the same time, some are developing truly global talent managers, whose pay scales are most pay level to similar manager in other companies than they are with typical rate of pay in either the firm's
headquarter country or its overseas locations.

Is one company achieves higher profits, it needs to raise higher wage to its all employees in nowadays HRM strategy? I feel that it depends on whether situations to make decisions to raise all employees' wages , due to it has higher profit reason in the year.

Robert, P.V. (2006) summarized these rules in dealing with subordinates, their performance should be enhanced. These rules includes using fair differential rewarding, it means that many managers try to treat all subordinates alike. When all employees receive equal rewards, superior performers begin to feel that their efforts are unappreciated, when poorer recognize that they won't be penalized for minimal effort. In response, over time, most above-average performers will drop their performance to the minimal level.

A few superior performers may persist absolutely , but most will lower their efforts to the level that they feel equals their rewards. So, when rewards are commensurate with performance, however, subordinates receive a quite different message. Superior performers get the signal that their efforts are valued, and potentially high performers are encouraged to try harder, identifying valued rewards for individual , it means that if a manager hopes to influence an employee's behavior through the use of rewards, the rewards must have value to the employee. One of the best ways to obtain such information is simply to ask employees what rewards they could like to receive. Younger workers may prefer more paid vacation days, ( non-monetary value reward) or greater participation in decision making ( high position management role) . The older workers may choose better medical insurance or a longer contribution to their pension plan, instructing subordinated on how rewards are tied to performance. It means that in order for maximizing organization's effectiveness, employees must clearly understand how rewards and performance are connected. When specific information is lacking, subordinates may try to second-guess their manager's intentions by constructing their own imagined system of rewards. Thus, much under productivity can be avoid of a manager clearly states goals for performance and explains how rewards will be related to performance, providing information feedback on performance means that in order to meet their manager's standards of performance, employees must have instructive feedback. Their manager must evaluate their information for them, indicating how well or how poorly they are doing and suggesting specific ways to improve. In addition to providing guidance, feedback can also serve as an additional form of suggestion.

Thus, when an organization earns higher profit, it seems that it ought not raise all employees salaries to be higher, because some hard working employees will feel unfair if the lazy employees can raise the same salary level to same to the hard working employees in the year. On the consequence, the hard working employees will be possible to under productivity or productivity in below level efficiency or inefficiency to perform their unsatisfactory or disagreed feeling to complain whose employers. Then, the organization will encounter low productivity in possible. Hence, fair reward management plan to all employees which is needed in any organization.

What are IT and bank and property management and school organizations nowadays reward management system characteristics ?

In IT and bank and property industries which need reward strategic reasons: Reward management systems have major impact on organization capability to catch, retain and motivate high potential employees and as a result getting the high level of performance. I also believe reward of employee performance can lead to differentiation between the productivity of the bank employees. In fact, bank employee performance is originally what on employee does or does not do. Performance of employees could include quantity of output, quality of output, timeliness of output, presence at work, cooperativeness.

Reward management in bank service industry, bank organization needs have effective and attractive reward management system to attract talent human resource applications. But banks are facing global saving bank competition. Reward management system is a core function of human resource discipline and is a strategic partner with company management. An good reward management can raise bank service employees performance in loan, saving mortgage etc. different departments. An effective reward management system can shorten service timeliness to raise talent employee individual bank service performance, raise the talent employee team cooperative effort in loan, mortgage, counter etc. different service departments.

However, reward management system tool includes both financial and non-financial rewards which are also called as extrinsic and intrinsic rewards. In bank industry financial rewards include salary increase, bonus, commission, housing loan allowance, education loan allowance. The non-financial rewards include promotion and title, authority and responsibility, appreciation and praise, participation to decisions, vacation time, comfort of working place, social authority, customer and management positive oral and written feedback, flexible working hours, design of work recognition , social rights, etc.

Property management industry reward management practitioners include property managers, caretakers, attendants, security guards, facility maintenance workers and cleaners. It is essential for employers to formulate strategic plans and coordinate labor relations of human resource with the development. In responds to the people-related challenge and opportunities to property management industry. It includes six aspects: communicating and improving staff benefits, promoting work-life balance and health and enhancing work arrangements, enhancing staff's career development and promotion prospect, improving the professional image of the industry, friendly employment practices for mature persons. Through these practices enterprises can make their job vacancies about attractive and answer misunderstandings about the property management industry.

Thus, the manpower shortage challenge will be avoid , when the people have interest to join the industry and they feel the reward is attractive to them to develop career. How to improve staff benefit? It includes new recruit entry bonus schemes, giving out little gifts and bonuses, during celebrations and festive occasions, and granting gratuities to critically ill employees or on the death of the employee's immediate family members, offers employees insurance plans, offering award schemes for employee's children by granting scholarships to outstanding students in recognition of their excellent exchange scholarships are available to subsidize their children's study abroad, promoting working-life balance to staff, such as organizing interest classes, setting up sports teams, organizing gatherings, participating in charitable activities, encouraging employees to organize social gatherings, promoting happiness at work, strengthening occupational safety and health arrangements to employees, e.g. setting up occupational safety and health committee / departments, formulating occupational safety and health policies, entertainment of work arrangement: compressed working days, five-day work week, flexible working days, flexible rostering, job sharing, part time work pattern, most rest time for frontline employee, job nature or workflow modification / re-engineering, improvement of employee's workplace environment, intra-district redeployment.

Reward is an important element in information technology industry. The IT industry had been needing a leader in changing traditional compensation strategy. Pay for performance needs to be designed effective reward system to encourage IT employee to work hardly in order to reward and contribute the most to an IT organization's technological productivity and profits.

The compensation mix depends on deliverable and the impact it has on the IT business. Consequently higher the responsibility greater the variable content in the pay package. IT industry has many IT professionals , such as programmers, software or hardware engineers, e-commerce website designer etc. different IT professionals. Hence, different IT professionals need have different skills to evaluate pay performance level fairly. However, performance related pay plans, it is a motivator the improves productivity. It helps in improving IT product productivity and performance levels when making every IT professional individual equally to encourage or motivate them to work to hardly in their IT unique professional aspects. It is a greater motivator for top performances and teams as they can get fair and reasonable reward and pay according to their contributions.

In fact, there is no standard formula for a performance -related incentive plan, it is unique for each IT professional. However, the incentive plan should need to be design to each IT professional with an organization's objectives. They include, communication and understanding of objectives, consideration of different IT professional performance against objectives, translating evaluation into the kid of IT professional performance rating, a link between ratings and pay to the kind of IT unique professional skill.

University HR strategic reward management system( review promote monitor scheme) aims to improve systems and skills for teaching employee communication, support teaching management to play a move active role in communication key messages, ensure school reward policies and procedures are fair to teaching staffs and administrative non-teaching staffs in salary rank increasing level, establish improved consultation procedures at academic and teaching service level, demonstrate the values and ethics by the university through management practices and communication with teaching staffs and non-teaching staffs, improve the profile and performance of the university by recruiting and developing talent teaching employees with appropriate external recognition , certain academic disciplines present more different recruitment challenges and profile of the university as an employer could be improved in the academic labour market, recruiting sample of selection decisions through early stages of employment to assess quality of appointment and identify learning points, support and encourage recruitment messages to improve selection practice including skills and high quality appointment decisions, raise the profile of the university as an employer regionally, nationally and internationally, establish succession planning for all key roles and positions linked with clear career progression with job families, to face in a difficult economic climate the university needs to continue to attract and keep high quality staff to work in an efficient and cost effective manner. The extension of workload allocation models to all academic units is an important tool to assist in managing workload fairly and more effectively, well targeted and designed training and development is very effective in motivating and enabling staff and support productivity.

What advantages do nowadays reward strategy brings to nowadays organizations?

Reward strategy can be applied to large organization, it can be also applied to small organization, e.g. family business, family business also needs compensation policies, the result encourages professional growth among family members and other employees as well as strategic business goal accomplishment. In general, compensation can be divided into the categories of base pay ( equity as a basic for fairness , benefit, e.g. health care insurance, salary , wages, incentive compensation ( e.g. bonuses, deferred compensation, stock or share options) and perks e.g. club membership, use of the company's private mountain, beach for holiday entertainment or sport activities e.g. free golf sport and company 's automobiles to provide to employees to drive in their private time.

Craig, E. A (2011) indicated that although small business has less employees , but it also needs compensation adjustments. The reasons include: (1) performance-based increases i.e. a rise, (2) annual wage adjustments e.g. cost of living increases to remain with what comparable businesses are paying and corrective adjustments to more pay for a position into with other position in the business increases are considered to be a key component of compensation by managers and non-management employers alike. The difference between one small organization's and one large organization's performance based increase is possible that one large organization has more a rise amount of performance -based increases in every time performance review. Otherwise, one small organization has less a rise amount of performance -based increases in every time performance review.

A good reward strategy can develop a philosophy of compensation that builds a framework for base pay and incentive tailored to the special values, goals, and needs of the particular family firm. Hence, one family or small firm's compensation -reward strategy can be explained to be needed, due to these factors : the firm can compare pay and performance levels with those of businesses with whom which compete for employees, the firm's goal is to provide total compensation between median and the percentage of comparable groups, base salary will be made more accurate decision at or high or below the median level for the comparable groups, individual salaries will be made more accurate decision within how much percent of the midpoint for the firm's comparison group's salary range, the firm can make more accurate decision on emphasizing whether performance -based incentives ought be spent at the expense of the salary, whether annual incentives ought be exceed those of comparably sized competitors, whether long-term incentives ought be based on results that add shareholder value.

However, culture can influence some business owners how to make compensation issues, culture means beliefs, values, assumption, habits and behavior patterns of the organization. The reasons staffs are paid the way, they are may be partly unconscious and may arise from the personal and family history and the deeply felt personal needs of the business leader or leaders. So, any family or small business will ought try to develop a philosophy of compensation ( reward) strategy , which may learn a great deal about itself in the process. For example, a entrepreneur has confidence in her or his ability to manage compensation on a case-by-case basis and maintain tight personal tight personal control over each individual pay, perks, incentives, dividends, and gifts in order to encourage its employees can raise more effort to increase the sale number to its different kinds of product in its shop. Otherwise, if a family member working in this kind of culture asks for a raise, the business owner will not talk to about how to raise compensation to his/her salespeople in Christmas period. Hence , culture seems to influence the large organization and small organization how to make itself compensation to salespeople in Christmas period.

However, a basis for fairness to base pay which can let the large organization or small organization's staffs to feel, it is very important , when the large or small organization needs to focus on filling a vacancy and getting new skills into key areas quickly to meet customer needs with quality and efficiency. Because if the large organization or small organization expects it sale turnover may increase or staff turnover may decrease, but hiring needed talent may become more difficult, indicating that the company's pay structure may have lost internal logic if it's basic pay is unfair to attract talent staffs choose to join to its organization to work, when they feel that the organization's base pay is not reasonable to compare its competitors ( pay for one job compared to another), and comparable jobs outside the company, the process is logical , objective and fair to be needed to judge the base pay structure to any organizations. Having a consistent, explainable ration for how compensation or reward is critical for employee and shareholders judgements about fairness. Hence, individual employee will usually compare his/her job in the company's salary and his/her similar job in another company's salary whether whose salary is same or more or less between whose company salary and similar company salary. Hence, a company needs to establish equitable base pay in a market value and merit system, with any adjustments , pay raises being a function of performance merit in order to make more reasonable compensation or reward to let its staffs to feel to avoid staff turnover number raises.

A rational compensation system steps can include: creating job description for all jobs, conducting a job evaluation to rank order jobs and determining which jobs that are similar in their importance to the business, obtaining external wage and salary survey information for representation jobs, utilizing other sources for comparable external data when needed, determining the company's reward strategy for compensation and deciding whether it wants pay to be set at the market average , whether it wants compensation at levels above or below the market average, or whether it wants to make a culture statement with pay levels, creating a wage and salary structure of starting pay levels, ( minimums ) and levels of pay for the most experienced workers ( maximums). Analyzing current pay levels against the new structure pay levels against the new structure to determine which jobs are paid appropriately and which ones are not, considering individual, unique jobs that may have qualitative more or less important than external market comparable might suggest, making pay adjustments for those that are not of the range, accelerating regular increases for positions below the target range and decelerating or not making increased that are above the range. Finally , it needs to periodical check or review the wage and salary structure against outside bench market ( external similar competitors positions to maintain external equity).

The point factor job evaluation tool can help the organization to make decision whether the staff ought pay how much salary level is the most reasonable. The point method include the elements such as : The experience element means the factor appraises the length of time normally required for an individual to acquire the necessary knowledge and ability to affectively perform the duties of the job. The experience level element means that whether the worker individual working experience in the firm, e.g. up to three months, he/she can earn the lowest points, till to comprehensive over right years, he/she can earn the highest points. The direction of others element means this factor appraises the responsibility to the job , it includes for organization, selection , assignment , guidance and review of personnel and the performance of other supervisory tasks. The direction of others level can indicate the employee earns none points when whose jobs involves no responsibility or authority for the direction of others, till to the highest points when the employee can confirm to own administrative ability,whose job is responsible for general administrative or executive supervision of all or broad segment of company operations as well as he/she can establish general policies and procedures and formulates and applies broad plans of operations.

Compensation specialists can help the company to select representative jobs from a company and find good external comparisons. They will need to make adjustment. Some criteria for determining a jobs' market value can include position title and job description, industry, size of company, sales or revenue volume, cost of living, based on location etc. data to determine whether their company's salary level is acceptable or reasonable to a job's market value. They need to gather the data concerns the job's market value. This is helpful because the latest supply and demand factors can affect certain positions may not show up in surveys. They must need to gather similar industry's organization size, sale or revenue volume data, daily cost of living and transportation cost how to influence their employees' income and similar competitors' employees income in order to make more reasonable and accurate salary structure adjustment.

Why does Reward management can bring positive influence to work performance as well as how to achieve high work performance to nowadays organizations?

How can reward management strategy raise job performance? In organization, work performing is affected by job characteristics and physical work environment, ability and skills and the willingness to performance to the individual employee. The major strategic rewards decisions to reward employees which include: What to pay employees, how to pay individual employees, cognition programs? Concerning about what to pay? The employer needs to establish a pay structure balance between internal equity, ( the value of the job for the organization) and external equity , the external competitiveness of an organization's pay relative to pay in its industry.

What does reward management mean? The management discipline is concerned with the formulation and implementation of strategies and policies, the purpose of which are to reward employees fairly, equitably and consistently in accordance with their value to the organization. It deals with design, implementation and maintenance reward systems ( processes, practices, procedures) that aim to meet the needs of both the organization and its stakeholder. Thus, total reward can include non-financial as well as financial element is developed, implemented and treated. Usually , the components of total reward include two aspects: tangible rewards ( base pay, contingent pay and employee benefits ) as well as relational intangible rewards (learning and development), the work experience and achievement, growth , non-financial rewards . Then, it is the total reward. However, reward can include these tangible and intangible elements: payment, such as salary, bonus, shares etc. Praise, such as positive feedback, commendation, staff-of -the year award etc. Promotion, such as status, career development. Punishment, such as disciplinary action, criticism, withholding pay. Thus, if one employee can not achieve the satisfactory performance, he/she ought need to get disciplinary action to be punished in order to let he/she learns how to revise his/her performance to raise working efficiency.

How to implement strategic reward management? Where do we want our reward practices to be in a few years time ( vision)? How do we intend to get these ( mean)? So, a declaration of intent that defines what the organization wants to do in the longer term to develop and implement reward policies, practices and processes, that will further the achievement of its business goals, and need the needs of the stakeholders, it can give a framework to other elements of rewards. So, the structure and content of a reward strategy may include: Environment analysis, macro-level, social, economical, demographic, industrial level, and micro-level competitors, analysis of job evaluation, financial conditions, gap analysis.

When the organization expected to apply reward strategy to raise employee individual performance successfully? It needs to know what job evaluation means. It is a systematic process for defining the relative worth/size of the jobs roles within a organization, for establishing internal relatives, for designing an equitable grade structure and grading jobs in the reward structure. For example, reward strategy can attempt to reduce wage gaps, when the wage gap can occur in the company, it can use international benchmarking in job evaluation. However, the cause is simple. The market of top managers is usually international, they earn international wage, or they leave the firm. The market of workers with little or no qualification is local in nearly every case. They can earn local wages. In less developed countries , this can lead to raise wage gaps between the top and bottom employee. Hence, if the firm discovered it has large distance of wage gaps between its top and bottom level positions. It ought need to find methods to adjust these positions' salaries to be reduce large distance of wage gaps fairly in order to let these large distance of wage gaps of position employees , they can feel their company is more fair to treat every employee.

Moreover, firm also need to consider that whether it ought choose which type of individual payment to excite its employee individual performance to be improved. They may include: performance -related increases basic pay or bonus -related to assessment of performance, contribution-related pay is related both to inputs and outputs, skilled-base pay is related to high or low skilled to the individual effort performance, service -related pay is related to whether the employee needs to spend how long service-time to satisfy customer's need in order to measure every service employee's performance, team-based pay is related to team performance, it can encourage teamwork, loyalty and cooperation and it can be demotivating on individual level.

All of these any types of reward method will improve or encourage the low performance employee individual working efficiency or raise productivity more easily as well as fair reward strategy can upgrade the high performance employee individual efficiency or encourage them to exceed their productive level or raise their productivity to achieve the maximum number. Hence, reward management has direct relatively to influence every employee's performance in order to bring either long term positive or negative influence to their organizations.

What factors can influence organization's past traditional and present reward strategy changes ?

What is reward management strategic principle to employment relationship? employees needs to pay tangibles ( salary, wage, cars, educational , holiday allowance etc.) or/and intangible ( recognition, career development growth etc.) rewards to employees aim. Individual balance to achieve tangible output, sales and/or intangibles loyalty , service performance, commitment. Hence, reward management forms the employment relationship, if an HR manager is to succeed in successfully managing the employment relationship, he/she will have to do well in reward management.

The reward management principle includes simplicity, it must be easily understood by everyone in the organization, fairness and equitability , every component of the system must be justifiable applied. This element is arguably the most challenging to implement and is the cause of most reward management related problems , such as strike, turnover, dissatisfaction etc. Hence, an attractive communication and training to the low skillful labour to have chance to upgrade high skillful which is needed, a participatory chance is effective one should ideally be negotiated and agreed between management and employees.

In fact, traditionally companies have always adopted the base pay strategy. It pays the legal minimum wages and salaries. However, it does not adequate in new work cultures and in terms of attracting , retaining and motivating top performers for strategic purposes, but still very commonly for lower level employees. The new reward strategic options include as below:

1. Knowledge and skills based strategy, because of the proven relation job performance, organizations have sought to encourage continuous skills development by trying it to rewards. A organization simply varies its pay structure according to one's level of knowledge and skill ( job evaluation systems. It can define which skills, it values and will pay for and must have a supportive training and development strategy. It is based pay with an equal base pay and a variation based on skills and knowledge. It may be costly in the short-term , but it is beneficial from a knowledge HR base through increased productivity and quality of product.

2. Performance based ( varied pay based structure strategy), employees should be rewarded only for the value they create. A company will reward employee in the same grade variably depending on each employee's performance.

3. Incentive based pay structure strategy, it measures but being different in that it focuses on group performance rather than individual performance. The starting point in strategy is to define group performance targets , such as productivity sale volumes or profitability.

What factors can influence organization's reward strategy? They include: Affordability, the argument is that an organization can't borrow to reward employees, but it should reward from the value created by the employees themselves; legislation sets the minimum base pay minimum fixed pay rate; union/workers committees' pay level are determined through collecting bargaining. For example, strike issue will bring higher salary level in possible; external job value, the market value of the job, e.g. what is the market value of an HR manager or clerical assistant; internal job value, perceived value of job compared to the other jobs which the organization will determine the reward for the jobs , e.g. HR manage compared to finance manager; value of the person, employees holding similar jobs can be paid differently depending on the value to the organization performance; the economy changing factor ( labor supply/demand) in labor market, e.g. it is a depressed economy increases the supply of labour, it will reduce the labour wage/salary market prices, due to the economy is bad , employers won't need to raise to any employees number and it has excess labour supply number to affect reward policy strategy.

Why does reward system of McDonald need to be changed?

Beccause Mc Donald's organizations are expanding to global , so its employees and customers number must increase. In order to adopt its

organizational change. It must need to
change its reward system in order to satisfy its employees' psychological and reward needs. For McDonald's Corporation U.S. employees at corporate, division and region offices, McDonald benefits are organized into four Performance management includes processes that effectively communicate , company aligned goals, evaluate employee performance and reward them fairly.

Your Pay and Rewards (ref from McDonald's reward system).Attractive program follows a "pay for appearance" beliefs: The better your results, the greater your pay opportunities.

· Base Pay

Since employees' bottom pay is the most important portion of their recompense, McDonald's maintain the competitiveness of our base pay through an annual review of both external market data and interior peer data. In our business, division and region offices, McDonald's has a broad banding compensation system. Broad banding allows for suppleness in terms of pay, movement and growth.

· Incentive Pay

Inducement pay gives our workers with the possibility to earn spirited total compensation when performance meets and exceed goals. For our corporate, parting and region office, the Target Incentive Plan (TIP) links employee presentation with the presentation of the business they hold up. TIP pays a gratuity on top of employees' base salaries base on business presentation and their person appearance.

· Long Term Incentives

Long term incentives are granted to entitled workers to both prize and retain key employees who have shown continued presentation and can crash long-term value creation at McDonald's. for the befits of employees the long term incentives are very helpful because when the organization has a policies of incentives or long term incentives then the employees of the organization feel secured and work hardly for the organization. Similar like this any company or any Originations rewarding system always brought positive crash.

· Recognition Programs

Mc Donald's recognition programs are intended to reward and recognize physically powerful performers. For our corporate, separation and region offices, these take in the president Award (given to the top 1% of individual performers worldwide) and the Circle of fineness Award (given to top teams worldwide to be familiar with their aid for advancing our vision). Once start to hesitation your honesty, and then no one is leaving to alter their activities Appraisal system is also very helpful and makes a positive competition and encouragement in between the employees of the organization. Promotions will be appraisal based which encourage employees for hard work.

- Company Car Program

Mc Donald's company car program provides entitled employees with a company car for both business and individual / personal use. If entitled, employees can decide from. This is also very encouraging and motivating incentive for employees. It creates competition between employees and they work hard to get this incentive.

In conclusion, the assumptions the company is creation about their prospect service and its intention to support their progress. Practical processes for deploy people and delivering enlargement which are consistent with these intention. The reserve and promise for taking these types of program used. If we see in past we can get that simple ways in which the company could use the out test for the planed strategies and special and important clues for the good results.

CHAPTER THREE

# Human resource role nowadays changes

What is past HR role in organizations?

HR role in business functions: HR ethics and code of industry includes that HR people should act legally, ethically and professionally as these aspects: Act legally, it represent the most core of obligations. HR is responsible for keeping current with changes in employment law and keeping management informed of risk or possible library. Act ethically, HR represents all employees at all levels of the organization, regardless of sex, age , race , color, material status, religion, disability or other protected class. At the same time, HR promotes the ethical culture of an organization. They must model the highest level of ethical behavior, administer all company policies and procedures fairly in handling disciplinary.

HR must conduct thorough investigations and make recommendations or decisions based on facts. Act professionally, HR must keep employees' and companies' information in the strictest confidence and protect company information when dealing with employees or individuals outside of company. HR must follow changes in employment law, company policies and employment issues. They are also responsible for continuing education to remain expects in the field to be a successful strategic business partner. HR staffs need own business knowledge and understand the cost of people-related activities and responsible for measurement to all HR programs and processes, subject matter expert, in this role, the HR person should passes HR knowledge in relation to the most up-to-date employment law at the best HR practices for sourcing and staffing, remuneration strategy and systems, performance management, employee relations, and people development and advice business as appropriate.

At all time, a professional HR will keep his/her management informed of any potential risk and liability to the business , due to the change of employment law. Creating good working environment, HR needs to motivate , engage, contribute good and happy working environment to le staffs to work in the organization. HR needs to help to establish and promote the organizational culture in which people are willing to do the best performance to the jobs, and commit customer's needs and concerns.

In this role, the HR person identifies and facilitates overall talent management strategies, employee development opportunities, employee assistance programs, long term incentive and effective communication opportunities and channels between management and employees. HR is such as one change agent. The HR person needs to know how to link changes to the strategic needs of the organization and being able to show empathy and concern employee needs to minimize employee dissatisfaction change. So, HR person needs have the ability to execute successful change strategies.

HR functions in organization include: workforce planning, sourcing staffing, organizational development, skills training , learning , talent development, reward management, compensation and benefits, employee relations, communication, engagement, HR policy and legal recommendation, change management, employee welfare, workplace health and safety.

Staffing sourcing means the success plan or buy recruit from external. It is a process , a company ensures that employees are recruited and developed to fill the key roles. Through high-performing employees, develop their knowledge, skills and capability and prepare them for advancement or promotion into even more challenging roles in 3 to 5 years‘ time. So, it asks to develop the employees to special projects, team leadership roles, internal and external movement to training and development opportunities.

The success plan should identify key position, its key roles and contributions, key success factors of key positions, skill, knowledge, capabilities, reasons cause of turnover, potential success identification, development plans for potential successor to reach the required success factors.

Recruit from external or buying recruiting resource from the labour market is suitable to meet company short-term staffing needs for the junior to middle level positions. It can help new skills and new experience. Sources of supply can be from a combination of full time/part time employees, recruitment agencies' temporary workers and contract workers.

The contracting applicants arrangement stage means the HR needs to contract the job applicants and invite for an interview, conducts the job interview, prepares the resume in advance and highlight areas to require further during the interview, knowledgeable about the company, the role in discussion and the job application process the applicants able to answer questions they might have, enthusiastic , friendly and courteous , so the applicant will be viewed the opportunity move positively, resourceful and helpful to hire managers , such as sharing tips ar interviewer, how to manage interviewees' expectation etc.

Arranging interview stage providing the shortlisted candidates with helpful information about the interview includes: when and where the interview, who will be in the interview, how the interview will be conducted. Facilitating effective interview, the interviewer needs to ensure the interviewing environment is comfortable one free no noise, not leave the candidate waiting for too long. When closing the interview, the interviewer should advise the candidate of the possible must steps, online screening of application forms, using online to search and compare job applicant's information, job skills, years of experience, education level to identify suitable candidates for further selection processes.

Reward management is concerned with the formulation and implementation of strategies and policies that aim to reward people fairly, equitably a fact, employers nowadays can hardly rely solely on base salary to attract and motivate their employees. More emphasis has other benefits , such as retirement benefits and learning opportunities. Performance and reward system should be market-based, equitable and cost-effective. Rewards do not only depend on skills, capabilities and experience of individuals, but also performance. In order to encourage top rate performers, employers must not only offer rewards for good work, but they must also have consequences for substandard work. Although, employers usually do not want to follow through with negative consequences, it is sometimes a necessary process. Otherwise, employees have no incentive to correct unacceptable behavior.

Employers also needs to clearly know about what is recognized by the company and how these will be measured. So that they understand the relationship of performance and reward. Total reward may include anything value resulting of employment relationship to the employee with a goal to attract, motivate and attract talent. It can include financial and non-financial rewards and that these can change over time depending on their personal circumstances. Employers need to find out what attracts, engages individuals and explore how best they can meet these needs. It is important that the company how design's the elements of the reward package to support.

What factors can determine rewarding for performance, qualification, experience, potential, behavior, effort, achieving goals, meeting targets. How the employees will be rewarded, the awards whether are company's work culture/characteristics are whether driven the right behavior/ performance/efforts the awards are be valued by the employees, the awards are how often to be given, how often the rewards are reviewed, the award is long or short term.

Legal framework for reward system , such as payment of wage, restriction on wages deduction, minimum wage, benefit, such as share options or housing benefits. Major benefit plans may include: retirement benefit schemes, personal security, e.g. healthcare, dental , hospitalization, accident or life insurance, financial assistance, e.g. mortgage interest subsidies, rental subsidies, staff discount, education subsidies, personal needs, e.g. holidays and leave with pay child care, fitness and facilities, use of holiday house, employee shares purchase plan, company car etc. welfares.

What is nowadays HR's role in corporate social responsibility?

The HR function should help formulate and achieve environmental and social goals when also balancing these objectives with traditional financial performance metrics. The HR function can serve as a partner in determining what is needed or what is possible in formulating corporate values.

At the same time, HR should play a key role in ensuring that employees implement the strategy consistently. For example, encouraging employees, through training and compensation to find ways to reduce the use of environmentally damaging chemicals in the products, assisting employees in identifying ways to recycle products that can be used for play grounds for children who do not have access to healthy places to play designing a company's HRM system to reflect equity development avoid well-being , thus contributing to the long-tem health.

How HR policies shape the workplace and how HR can improve employee well-being through better working conditions and more positive workplace a cultures. Top-management can encourage particularly supervisory support, also has been identified as key to employee environment actions. In addition, adopting HRM and communicating a pro-environmental image can have a positive reputational effect. This helps to staff , the company leading to lower recruitment and training costs and a better financial bottom line. In fact, in some cases, a pro-environmental stance may be more important to potential employees. It can help a company address wider social problems that are affecting not only its external community, but also the company's financial bottom line. For example, The US postal service employees participate in more than 80 cross-functional teams across the US do drive energy reduction and resource conservation. These teams helped the postal service reduce energy, water, solid waste to landfills and petroleum fuel use as well as recycles more than 222000 tons of material. Thus, HR-related activities that can support , such as responsible workplaces, human rights, safety practices, labor standards, performance developments, diversity, employee compensation and more.

What is nowadays Human resource role in Hong Kong business organizations?

Andy, W.C. el.(2002) indicated that economic
downturn which began in early 1998 had dramatic effects on Hong Kong's prosperity and increasing rates of Gross Domestic Product, especially during the 1990s and the early years of the 21st century. In late 2002s, Hong Kong's unemployment rate stood at 7 per cent and showed no immediate prospect of diminishing. This has huge implication for human resource professionals and especially for their training, as managers of the organization's most precious resource, its people. Moreover, downsizing and consequent increases in the rate of unemployment were logical consequences of this process.

However, Hong Kong's strengths in finance, trade, services and tourism provided benefits from the effects of these recessionary forces. But, Hong Kong was faced with the poor of dealing with the human resource implications and other aspect of workforce reduction. Hence, it explains why HK organizations need to consider HRM functions as part of the acquisition, development , motivation and maintenance of human resources in order to bring direct relevance of the strategic decision-making on which profits and productivity depend.

Human resource management is focused on the development and application of policies in relation to human resource planning, recruitment, selection, placement, and termination, management education , training and career development, terms of employment and methods and standards of remuneration, working conditions and employee services, formal and informal communication and consultation through employer and employee representative at all levels, negotiation and implementation of agreements on wages and working conditions , as well as procedures for the avoidance and settlement of disputes and the creation of a fairer and more equitable workforce in which discrimination in any form is viewed as unethical behaviors.

HRM responsibilities include to conduct research into local wage levels to ensure the firm's reward system is competitive with those in other companies, devising remuneration systems to excite or encourage or persuade workers into enhanced effort and efficiency, administering superannuation schemes, e.g. retirement welfare plan, and advising employees about their pensions, maintaining personnel records and statistics, preparing accurate job descriptions and other retirement documentation, implementing health and safety regulations, accident prevention and the provision of first-aid facilities, e.g. safe construction site environment, designing and evaluating management training and development schemes linked with succession planning and developing and implementation systems with facilities organizational communication.

Role of HR manager includes the control function, such as analysis of key operational data in human resource areas of labor turnover, wage cost, absenteeism, monitoring of staff performance ( staff appraisal ) and recommending appropriate remedial action to managers; the advisory function offers expect advice on human resource policies and procedures, e.g. which employees are ready for promotion, who should attend a certain training course, arrangement contracts of employment, health and safety regulations etc. related human resource related issues.

The future role of HR manager needs to concern to adopt an international insight in their work, growing concern for the application of ethical approaches to human resource management, implementation of equal opportunity , data privacy, and arranging flexible working models, such as job sharing, job rotation, permanent part –time work, increased awareness to encourage or persuade for effective employee participation in company production systems in order to achieve raising efficiencies and effectiveness, concerning the consequences for HR management of the ageing workforce discussed issues, such as prolonging / shortening working age or shortening /prolonging retirement age policy, participating legal system in human resource issues, including laws on hiring , dismissing, equal opportunities, age, country discrimination conduct of industrial relations.

HR planning can help management in making decision in the following areas: recruitment. , avoidance of redundancies ( increasing labor turnover, training, management and development, estimates of labor cost, productivity bargaining, raising effectiveness or efficiency , accommodation requirements. In order to achieve company's maximum benefits purpose, HR planning needs continuous readjustment ( annual review) , because the goals of an organization are subject to change and its internal and external environment is uncertain. It is also complex because it involves to many independent variables, e.g. increasing skillful immigration job seeker number to compete in the country's local labor market or decreasing skillful labor, e.g. computer programmers, doctors, accountant, lawyers etc. occupation professionals sudden emigrate to other countries to seek jobs, consumer demand increases or decreases to the product. Hence , it must include feedback because if the plan can not be achieved, the objectives of the company will have to be modified so that they are feasible in human resource terms.

The human resource plan process to one company is a cycle process. The first step may include that it needs to follow issues from corporate plan's strategies and objectives. The main points to be considered such as capital equipment plans, reorganization, e.g. centralization or decentralization, how to change in product or in output, marketing plans and financial limitations.

After it gathers the company's corporate

strategic plan data. Then, it will implement its
second step. This step may include three aspects:

· How to achieve the reasonable present utilization of human resources in particular: numbers of employees in various categories, estimation of labor turnover for each grade of employee and the analysis of labor effects of high or low turnover rates on the organization's performance, amount of overtime worked, amount of short time, appraisal of performance and the potential of present employees and general level of payment compared with that in other comparable firms. All these HR related data is essential to be recorded in accurate attitude.

· The external environment of the company analysis, such as recruitment position, population trends, local housing and transportation plans, government policies in education and retirement.

· The potential supply of labor analysis, such as effects of local emigration and immigration, effects of recruitment or redundancy in local firms, possibility of employing categories not now employed, for example outsource employees number, part time and semi-retired workers number and changes in productivity , working hours.

The final step is that HR planning needs to be achieved. It includes recruitment/redundancy program, training and development program, industrial relations policy and accommodation plan. The issues will appear in this plan, such as jobs which will appear, disappear or change, to what extent redeployment or retraining is possible, necessary changes at supervisory and management is possible, necessary changes and supervisory and management levels, training needs, arrangements for necessary and details of arrangements for handling any human problems arising from labor deficits or surpluses , e.g. early retirement or other natural wastage procedures. Following , it needs to give feedback , what will be possible modification to company objectives to company's corporate level to review its HR plan whether it can achieve company's objectives and strategic aims.

Human resource manager can be one human resource relation consultant to give recommendation how the organization should be better equipped to cope with the HR consequences of changed circumstances, careful consideration of likely future human resource requirements could lead the firm to discover new and improved ways surpluses might be avoided, it helps the firm to create and develop employee training and management succession program, some of the problems of managing change may be foreseen or consultations with affected groups and individuals can occur at an early stage in the change process and decision can be taken and by considering all the relevant , options, rather than being taken in crisis situations, management can assess critically the strengths and weaknesses of its labor force and HR policies, wasting or excess of effort among employees can be avoided and coordination to worker's efforts is improved to raise efficiencies and productive effectiveness.

What is nowadays HR changing role in bank industry ?

What is human resource (HR) role in organization? What factors can change to influence HR? They include workforce changes, globalization, ethics, organizational growth, increased accountability. These factors can influence HR's role change in the organization. So , when you assume be one HR manager, you need to concern : How have you used you awareness of internal and external changes to guide the decision making of your stakeholders ,e.g. discussing the impact of trends in workforce skills with function leaders? Which of your knowledge , skill, abilities or other characteristics have been useful in consulting with stakeholders?

Hence, HR role needs to understand the organizational goals and the role each function plays, serves of a cross-functional bridge. Locates talent throughout the global organization, identifies and supports need for resources or training, advices core functions on how with adapts to organizational strategy. Moreover, HR leaders need own knowledge of other business functions and whose organizations' business influences specific actions by HR , e.g. understanding the type of experts needed by R&D and future trends for that need. Also, the HR leader needs to know which of whose knowledge, skills, abilities or other characteristics have been useful in responding to this challenge?

HR also needs to consider how its organizational functions. They have disadvantages and advantages in order to achieve HR staff skill, talent to satisfy different departments' needs effectively and efficiently. Organizational structure has three types: Firstly, functional type advantages of easy to understand, specialization develop economies of scale, communication within function, career paths, fewer people and disadvantages of weak customer or product focus , potentially weak communication among function, hierarchical structure. Secondly, product type advantages of economies of scale, product team culture, product expertise and disadvantages of regional or local focus, more people, weak customer focus. Finally, geographic type advantages localization, quicker response time and disadvantages of fewer economic of scale, more people potential quality control.HR also needs to concern when it's company needs to implement outsourcing employment need rea third party contractors' successful outsourcing depends on choosing the right activities to outsource, cooperation of contractor's performance objectives with strategic requirements.

Confirmation of contractors' reliability, capacity, expertise and ethical behavior. So , when the organization feel it needs to employ outsource contractors. The HR has responsibility to lead and know how to apply whose ethical practices competency in contracting for HR services or performing , due diligence or organizational sourcing, e.g. taking steps to protect employee data. The HR leader or manager also needs to know which of his/her knowledge skills, ability or other characteristics has been useful in responding to this challenge.

Standard chartered had have good talent management strategies to train its staffs. The talent management at standard chartered bank (SCB) features include: Standard chartered bank has good performance appraisal or measurement strategy. By making it a global standard to conduct face-to-face performance appraisals every six months. SCB is reviewing its own performance management objectives to make sure that those objectives stay relevant and achievable. Being sensitive to different cultures by employing different appraisal methods, also show that SCB understands the importance of managers and staff identifying and dealing with real, actual problems in a way that is most familiar and effective to them. Through appraisal, SCB also classifies their employees into 5 categories ranging from high potentials to critical resources, then to core contributors, followed by underachievers and finally underperformers. By identifying areas in which they are lacking and act.

What are the relevance HR problem to bring bank crisis to SCB. SCB view of employees as human capital in the organization, it could have at least minimized the less to a certain extent. For one, discussions between employers and still could have been more open and problem issues could have been identified at an earlier stage inefficiencies in the organization would have been uncovered , influence their performance against regional offices. In a way, having a certain amount of centralized control through talent management would also enable the monitoring of its offices globally.

What are performance appraisal aims? Performance appraisal is the measurement of the effectiveness of an employee's job performance. The process is described as the collection and use of judgements, ratings, perceptions or more objectives sources of information to understand better the performance of a person, team, unit, business, process program in order to guide subsequent actions and decisions. The result or performance outcomes represent the contributions that an individual's job performance makers to an organization and its goals.

Performance appraisal focus on measuring or appraising the job performance of a individual, e.g. use of surveys or rating focus to assess and evaluate employee behavior. It brings the either positive or negative feedback to the employee in the performance view and the new goals for the next performance period may be discussed.

What is nowadays HR changing role change in India automobile industry ?

Human resource development (HRD) is the part of human resource management in any organizations. It deals with training employees in the organization when the industry feels it have need to upgrade skills to its staffs. It aims to let them to learn new skills distributing resources that are beneficial for the employee's task. For automobile industry in India example, India automobile sale companies will need effective HRD in their organizations if they expect to sell automobiles to global customers attractively.

Authors ( May, June 2014) from internet essay indicated the India automobile sector is divided in four different sector which are as follow: two wheeler, which comprise of mopeds, scooters, motorcycles and electric two-wheelers passenger vehicles which include passenger cars, utility vehicles and multi-purpose vehicles, commercial vehicles that are light and material heavy vehicles and three wheelers that are passenger carriers and product carriers.

Why do India automobile sale companies need to concern HRD? Authors ( May, June 2014) indicated the automobile industry is one of the key drivers that boost the economic growth to India. However, the year

2013-2014 has seen a decline in the industry's growth . High inflation , high interest rates, low consumer sentiment and rising fuel prices with economic slowdown and rising fuel reason for the downturn of the industry.

Except for the two wheelers, all other segments in the industry have been weakening. These is a negative impact on the automakers and dealers who offer high discounts in order to push sales. To match the decline in demand, automakers need good skillful of automakers to manufacturers attractive automobiles in order to attract foreign automobile buyers to choose to buy themselves any kinds of automobiles.

Despite the comprehensive market being under extreme burden, the luxury car market has observed a robust double digit like during the year 2013-2014, as a result of rewarding new launches at lower price points. Hence, foreign robust luxury cars competitors influence India automobiles sale number to be reduced. Hence, India automobile manufacturers felt automobile manufacturing workers' skills need to be train or improve in order to manufacture more comfortable and good design vehicles to satisfy future global automobile consumers' driving enjoyable needs.

In fact, India automobile industry employment opportunities will trend increase in the future with the number of vehicles available on the road today, the need and requirement for people who can fix these machines is fast increasing. The automobile jobs like automobile technician, car or bike mechanics are a great option. Becoming a diesel mechanic is also a significant alternative in India, auto labor market. Diesel mechanics are responsible for repairing and servicing diesel engines. As they are also required to repair engines of trucks and buses, other than cars. Even if communication with people instead of repairing cars in what interest to Indian, then Indian have opportunity of becoming a salesperson or sales manager in an automobile company. Career opportunities in automobile design, paint specialists, job on the assembly line and insurance of vehicles is also available.

Future India automobile industry employment trend is as the destination choice for design and manufacture of automobiles employers who need to automobile production skillful worker number will rise, because India manufacturing heavy vehicles, passenger vehicles, commercial vehicles automobile production skillful workers need number will rise.

Hence, India automobile sale employers will need have good human resource development model for the automobile companies, if they expect to raise automobile sale competitive effort in global automobile sale market.

At the implementation level, India executives of the automobile companies need to strengthen their training, net working and more towards providing a satisfactory human resource development climate for its automobile industry car production, design, repair, salespeople employees and suggest suitable changes and corrections in the policy decisions for management of automobile companies and policy makers. Hence, future HRD practices in automobile industrial organizations for India automobile companies aim to identify the HRD mechanisms implemented in the selected automobile companies to achieve the training function to be effectively managed in the automobile companies in order to raise automobile sale competition effort in global automobile market.

What is challenge of HRM in nowadays organizational department?

As a HR specialist, what are the challenges you may face and what HR intervention mechanisms would you consider using in an attempt to drive individual and organizational performance in a multinational company? Critically evaluate this question by utilizing the appropriate academic literatures.

The challenges of the HR specialist when there engage in attempt of increasing the individual and organizational performances in Multinational Companies through developing a set of HRM best practices, especially relating to employee recruitment and selection, performance management and staff retention. Since the organizations are multinational number of concerns are arises such as dealing cultural issues with the organizational goals as well as individual goals. Furthermore organizational behaviors and tools such as engagement, motivation and empowerment are basically highlighted; without those it is merely a dream to achieving the business goals. Basically Multinational companies are aiming profits and there for individual and organisational performance are very vital for their existence.

HR has been organized in a different ways over the years. Some functions have emphasized delivery by location or by business structure. In these models an integrated HR team has serviced managers and employees at specific location or with in specific businesses units, with some more strategic or complex tasks reserved for the corporate center. The degree to which these different arms of HR were centralized or co-located and the question of whether they were managed by the business unit varied. Within the HR teams, depending up on their size their might have been specialization by work area (especially for industrial relations in the 1960s and 1970s) or by employee grade or group (responsibility, say, divided between those looking after clerical staff from those covering production) The advancement of personal management starts around end of the 19th century, when welfare officers came in to being.

There are some organizations where HR is seen as a central, corporate function with little advancement to business units. Some other organizations position themselves in the opposite direction, with a very small corporate center and all the activity distributed to business units. The question of best structure is how the function best organizes itself between the pulls of centralization and the pushes of decentralization.(The changing HR functions).

The HR assumptions and HR practices observed in high performing firms are the key elements to the formation of the Best Practice theory. Employment security, selective hiring, self managed teams, high pay contingent on company performance, extensive training, reduction of status difference, and sharing information are the key element of the theory. However less concern about the organisational goals and culture are given as draw backs for the theory.

According to the "best fit theory" a firms that follows a cost leadership strategy designs narrow jobs and provides little job security, whereas a company pursuing a differentiation strategy emphasizes training and development. In other words this argues that all SHRM activities must be consistent with each other and linked to the strategic objectives of the business. HRM uses various technologies to direct employees behavior towards objectives and tasks that deliver approved organisational performance. Many organizations try to frame these 'levers' with an overall performance management system, and attach incentives and rewards to achievements of objectives and targets within this. HR will need to reduce employment expenses to help organizations to save income. Direct costs include: Recruitment costs (advertising, admin, etc.),Induction/training costs, other admin costs associated with new hires, Overtime/ cost of temporary workers, reduced productivity cost etc. which are related to HR expenses.

In conclusion, there is evidence to suggest that including the practice out line within this organisational behaviours and tools can used to drive organisational and individual performance in Multinational companies. It is essential to have suitable recruitment and selection process, performance Appraisal System and staff Retention plan to ensure the right people, In the right place, at the right time with right attitude. Training and development is also vital to improve HR performance. In addition HR Specialists role will be more specific when these techniques applying in to multi cultural environments where people perceptions and behavioral patterns are different from each other.

What is the nature of the employment relationship change in nowadays HR department ?

John, B. & Jeff, G. ( 6 edition, 2017) indicated Human resource management defines a distinctive approach to employment management, which seeks to achieve competitive advantage through the strategic deployment of a highly committed and capable workplace using an array of cultural, structural and personnel techniques. Also, human resource management is a strategic approach to managing employment relations which emphasizes that leveraging people's capabilities and commitment is critical to achieving sustainable competitive advantage or superior public services. This is accomplished through a distinctive set of integrated employment policies, program and practices in an organizational and societal context. Moreover, human resource management underscores the importance of people, only the " human factor" or labor can provide talent to generate value. It should draw attention to the notion of indetermination or uncertainty, which devices from the employment relationship: Employees have a potential capacity to provide the added value desired by the employer. It also follows from this that human knowledge and skills are a strategic resource that needs investment and skillful management. Moreover, in the environmental change factor influences to any organizations need to provide a role for HRM in improving an organization's performance in terms of overall sustainability.

· What is the nature of the employment relationship change in nowadays HR department ?

The nature of the social relationship between employers and the social relationship between employees and employer is an issues of central analytical importance to HRM. The employment relationship describes a relation between employees ( non-managers and managers) and their employer. Through the employment contract, inequalities of power structure both economic exchange ( wage or salary) and the nature and quality of the work performed whether it is routine or creative. They can be short-term, primarily but not economic exchange for a relatively well-defined set of duties and low commitment or they can be complex long-term relationships defined by a range of economic inducements and relative security of employment, given in return for a set of duties and a high commitment from the employee.

Airline services: the demands of emotional labor of employment relationship between airline and airline staffs.Positive emotion at work offers an apparent win to win situaton for airline organizations and individuals as it suggests that if a job or work is correctly designed, individuals will feel better and perform better. What was once a private act of emotion management is sold now as labor in the public contract jobs? What was once a privately negotiated rule of feeling or displaying is now set by th airline company's standard practices division. However, such as airline service waiter job, a private emotional system has been subordinated to commercial logic and it has been changed by whose airline employers.

· HR role in business maximizing efficiency method

John , H. ( 2013) described the work of police officers, we might discuss the functions of preventing come and catching criminals, the practices of patrolling, filling in report forms, breaking up disturbances, making arrests, and the qualities of commitment service. He also indicated police work is much more complicated than the brief suggestions and management work ( including the management of police work) is much more complex still. It is hard to describe the functions without detailing the practices or to make sense of the practices without involving the functions.

John, H. (2013) defined characteristics of management is responsibility for an organization or organization unit and for the work of its members. The unit might be anything from a small retail outlet with one or two shop assistants to large corporation with tens or even hundreds of thousands of employees, but most managers are directly responsible for managing the organization of a manage number of people, typically between two and twenty and of the various processes in which they are engaged. So, we have sales managers and production managers and marketing managers and IT managers etc. organizing the work of specialists. The at the level, of the business unit or agency or regional subsidiary, we have general managers whose jobs is to organize and coordinate the work of different specialist groups.

- What is Maximizing efficiency method different between traditional HR and nowadays HR department ?

Maximizing efficiency was a work study or time-and-motion to be exercise designed to calculate how the work could be most efficiently carried out. This involved the analysis of different possible divisions of different possible tasks of labour into specialized tasks. The optimization of the tools and machines, and the optimization of the physical movements, required to operate them, assuming workers well suited to the specified tasks concern. The optimized system would then be so as to become a standard requirement to be implemented with absolute regularity, so that the whole workplace operated as a machine. Workers would be selected with the skills and strengths to perform each specialised task, and trained to follow the standard procedures. They would be fairly paid for what was scientifically established to be a reasonable level of performance ( assuming they were well pay introduced, to encourage over- performance and punish (underperformance). Both owners or employee would benefits.

It indicated conclusion was that output was determined less by working conditions or incentive systems than by the informed social pattern of the work group. Feeling mattered and wherever managers took a personal interest in the workers, made them feel important and generated mutually supportive and cooperative environment, output are enhanced management. It seems was not about mechanical optimization processes, but about leadership and team dynamics. The management characteristics were however critical and with some rearrangement they can be summarized as follows: A strong people orientation, every body is treated s part of the team and just as an replaceable resource, flexibility and teamwork value driven value system is through the company.

· six situation factors can influence management's choice of nowadays HR strategy ?

Beer , M., et al. (1984) explained that HRM and the issue of management goals and specific HR outcomes. The Harvard framework consists of six basic components as below:

Beer, M., et al. (1984) indicated these six situation factors can influence management's choice of HR strategy. Firstly, situation factors include workforce characteristics, business strategy and conditions, management philosophy, labor market, unions , task technology , laws and societal values. Any one of situation factor can influence management's choice of HR strategy. The situation factor can bring influences to other two components. Stakeholder interests component means shareholders, management, employee groups, government, community, union as well as human resource management policy choices component, it means employee influence, human resource flow, reward system and works systems. It emphasizes that management' decisions and actions in HR management can be fully appreciated only if it is recognized that they result from an interaction between constraints and choices will be influenced by situational factor component and share holder interests components and long-term consequences component influences.

The human resource management policy choices component will influence the human resource outcomes component, it includes commitment, competence, cost -effectiveness. It means that it needs to understand the importance of management's goals, the HR outcomes of high employee commitment and competence are linked to longer term effects on organizational effectiveness and societal well-being.

The assumptions are built into the framework are that employees have talents that are rarely fully utilized in the workplace and that they show a desire to experience growth through work. The, the human resource outcomes component will influence the long-term consequences component. It includes individual well-being, organizational effectiveness and societal well-being . The long-term consequences distinguish between three goals: individual , organizational and societal. At the level of the individual employee, the long-term HR outputs comprise the psychological rewards that workers receive in exchange for their effort. At the organizational level, increased effectiveness ensures the survival of the firm. The societal level, as a result of fully utilizing people at work, some of society's goals ( for example, employment and growth are attained.

Finally, the sixth component is a feedback loop component, it is through which the outputs flow directly into the organization and to the stakeholders. However, long-term outputs can influence situational factors, stakeholder interests and HR management policy choices in cycle two way relationship.

· Knowledge management strategy needs at nowadays hotel industry

Hotels' realization led to the design and implementation of a computerized knowledge library that was accessible to every site manager in every hotel across the Australia/South pacific/ South East Asia region. The system was designed to initiate a long-term knowledge-sharing culture by making it easier to share value-added practices and processes, thus reducing wastage of time and resources through replication.

The problem- The knowledge library operated as a two way system whereby managers could both add ideas or effective innovative practices and find solutions to some of their own operational problems that demanded new ideas or innovation. To simplify its use, the system was designed to store ideas by hotel function ( that is food and beverage, housekeeping etc.) with both functional and key word search tools available , knowledge transfer was considered to have occurred once an idea had been implemented at another site.

Hotel management realized that they would need to create support systems to motivate sharing between the sites and geographical regions. This opened up an opportunity to achieve the desired knowledge, sharing actions and behaviors. Throughout the performance management system, as a result, for each site manager to pass their annual performance review, they had to retrieve a minimum of two ideas from the system and implement these in their hotel, as well as add two ideas to the system for others to be able to access and use.

The idea that the hotel different site managers' knowledge and expertise can play a strategic role in achieving competitive goals to expect to achieve a strategy results in superior performance, or a competitive advantage. Achieving high performance, improving employment skills, pay-for -performance, profit sharing, performance appraisal, team working, job evaluation, information-sharing, employment security, selective hiring, self-managed teams or team working, high pay contingent on company performance, extensive training, reduction in status differences, information sharing( knowledge management) benefits.

· Manpower planning role in nowadays HR department

Manpower planning ( workforce planning) means personnel and HR managers need to ensure that necessary supply of people was forthcoming to allow targets to be met. In theory at least, a manpower plan could show how the demand for people and their skills within an organization could be balanced by supply. The idea of a balance between demand and supply reflects the influence of the language of classical labor economics, in which movement towards an " equilibrium" serves as an ideal.

The utilization, improvement and preservation of an organization's human resources. The four stages of the planning process may include: the first stage is an evaluation or appreciation of the existing manpower resources. The second stage is an estimation of the proportion of currently employed manpower resources that were likely to be within the firm by the forecast data. the third stage is an essential or forecast of labor requirements needed if the organization's overall objectives were to be achieved by the forecast date and the fourth stage, it needs to measure to ensure that the necessary resources were available as and when required that is the manpower plan.

There were two main reasons for companies to use manpower planning. To develop their business objectives and manning levels and to reduce the " unknown" factor. Firstly organization implements strategy and targets, it brings organization practices and methods, it brings manpower review and analysis ( internal and external factors) , it brings forecast ( demand and supply), it brings adjust to balance ( recruit, retain and reduce).

Way of working includes: annualized hours, working time organized on the basis of the number of hours to be worked over a year rather than a week; it is usually used to fit in with peaks. Compresses hours, which allows individuals to work their total number of agreed hours over a shorter period. Flexi-time, employees have a choice about their actual working hours, usually outside certain agreed core times. Home working, either on a fully time basis or an a part time basis where employees divide their time between home and office. Job-sharing , which involves two people employed on a part time basis but, working together to cover a full time post. Shift-working , giving employers the scope to have their business open for longer periods than an 8 hour day. Staggered hours, employees can start and finish their day at different times. Term-time working, employees can take unpaid leave of absence during the school holidays.

· Recruitment, selection and talent management stages in nowadays HR department change may include:

Internal factors and external factors bring to workforce planning staffing needs options: internal via external brings to recruitment attraction via sources brings to applicant pool brings to selection assessment brings to job performance measurement brings to job analysis brings to workforce planning staffing needs opinions in cycle processing again.

Capable people who will apply for jobs within a organization. First, there is a need to attract people's interest in applying for employment. It implies that people have a choice about which organizations they wish to work for, even though during times of recession such choices might be limited. People may be capable of fulfilling a role in employment, but the extent to which this will be realized is not totally predictable. How capability is understood is increasingly determined by an organization's approach to talent management and development.

Under different labour market conditions, power in recruitment process will change between buyers and sellers of labour, the employers and employees respectively. Thus, in conditions of recession, employers are likely to reduce recruitment budgets and costs, paying more attention to developing the talent that has already been employed.

- Online recruitment

Budgetary factors will also affect how recruitment channels are used, with more use of online recruitment. For example, the ageing profile of the workforce around the world requires an adjustment of recruitment policies, the use of the internet and agencies for recruitment reflected to younger applicants, whereas older workers were more dependent on formal channels of recruitment, such as newspapers and journals. In addition, there have been many more graduates leaving university, and graduate employment is becoming very competitive. Many graduates will take longer to find employment that matches their skills. This might affect perceptions of the value to be gained from studying for a degree compared with the price of a degree.

There is a difference, however, in what recruiters think is important to this generation and what the generation itself thinks . Although HR policies will be designed to achieve particular organizational targets and goals, those policies will also provide an opportunity for individual needs and be satisfied . This view assumes that a fit between a person and the environment can be found so that their commitment and performance will be enhanced.

This an indication that the person to environment fit includes a person to organization fit, person to group fit and person to environment fit. If there is a match between the values within each of those areas expressed by the organization at the recruitment stage. The organization and the new recruits have a clear employees and can therefore manage those expectations.

HRM could help to shape the direction of change, influence culture and help bring about the mindset that would decide which strategic issues more considered. HR considerations, including the results of a review of the quantity and quality of people, the goals , objectives and targets whether they can achieve performance in an organization and for how work is organized into roles and jobs.

There has been a rapid growth in online recruitment , e-recruitment. As a result, organizations are advised to consider the design of websites and the terms that applicants might use to carry out job and vacancy searches. The usability of a company's website affects an applicant's perception of a job, with a focus on hyperlinks and text rather than graphic images and navigation links. However, issues with e-recruitment , including the one-way communication system, the fact that it is impersonal and passive, and the fact that it creates an artificial distance between the individual and the company.

· recruitment agent

However, once a recruitment strategy has been formed, an organization might outcomes its implementation to reduce costs and take advantage recruitment expertise, especial a large number of staff are recruitment. Recruitment agents act as "labor market inter-mediaties" between individual recruits and recruiting organizations. Financial service organization assessment and measurement of creating customer service performance indicators include as below:

Anticipating customer needs and planning accordingly, identifying the customers who will be of value to the company, recommending change to current ways of working that will improve customer service, arranging the collection of customer satisfaction data and acting on them. The analysis and definition of competencies should allow the identification and isolation of behavior that are distinct and are associated with competent or effective performance. On this assumption, the assessment of competencies is one means selecting employees.

Recruitment channels may include walk in, employee referrals, advertising, particularly online job boards, websites, labour market intermediaries, such as social media , social professional networks, recruitment agencies, educational associations, professional associations.

· job description

Job description includes job title, department, reponsible to , relationships, purpose of job/overall objectives, specific duties and responsibilities, physical and economic conditions as well as personnel specification includes physical characteristics, general intelligence, specific attitudes, interests, impact on other people, qualification and experience, abilities, motivation. Both job description and personnel specifications have been key elements, it replies too much on the analyst's subjective judgement in identifying the key aspects of a job and the qualities that related to successful performance.

· Selection

An organization wishes to recruit new employees to define criteria against which it can measure and assess applicants. Increasingly , such criteria are set in the form of competencies composed of behavioral characteristics and attitudes. Organizations have become increasingly aware of making good selection decisions, as selection involves a number of costs include: the cost of the selection process itself, including the use of various selection instruments, the future cost of training new staff , the cost of labor turnover if the selected staff are not retained.

There are good reasons why organizations need to consider the reaction of applicants to selection methods. If the selection is viewed as the attraction of the organization may be diminished, candidates who have a negative experience can dissuade others, a negative selection experience can impact on job acceptance , selection methods are covered by legislation and regulations relating to discrimination, mistreatment during selection will put off future applicants and may also stop applicants from buying the organization's products or using their services.

What is the role of HR technology change in nowadays organizations?

What is the role of technology in Human Resource Development? Identify some key forms of e-learning and critically evaluate their advantages and disadvantages, providing appropriate examples from organisations. It will define what Human Resource Development is and why it needs technology. Also it will discuss what electronic learning (e-learning) is, and will explain some key forms of e-learning and why we need to use e-learning. It will give a brief indication as to what technology actually is, and also the progression of technology. The essay will critically evaluate the advantages and disadvantages of using e-learning in Human Resource Development. There will be appropriate examples used to show how different organisations use e-learning within their company/organisation. Finally it will offer conclusions as to why I think technology should or should not be a part of Human Resource Development.

Why does HR development need technology?

Technology is always progressing and this is very good for companies who need or even sell technology. If we look at how a few years back within companies the secretary would need to file documents manually and this could take a long time, also apart from the time issue there were more serious problems like documents going missing or being damaged. This is where technology began to progress because there was a new technology progressing and this was the database and this could hold all the documents you needed safely onto the computer and that way it would be a lot faster and more secure for the secretary to file the documents. This is just one example there are many more ways in which technology has helped to progress companies. The example given here is just to show that technology is progressing and it will keep progressing much further in the future years to come.

Human Resource Development is all about learning, training, developing and education the employees in the workplace. There is a difference between these four concepts but there all correlated. If for example we looked at learning; this can be learnt anywhere and you can be learning yourself the new skills, but on the other hand if you looked at education you are being taught something but in a formal way but the two are linked because from both of these you are learning new skills and then you can go on to training and developing them skills.

HRD was not always known as this, there was a shift from welfare officers to HRD. HRD was initially set up for training and development and this was to help the employers in crafts such as electricians, or engineers as an example and from this they would be learning from their masters and will be developing their skills to be able to perform in the workplace. HRD created an integration of people management and development and this could become CIPD which stands for the chartered institute of personnel and development.

HRD likes to be strategic and is more for the organisation than the employees; it is also a long term method to help to build the company. HRD does like to implement change into their methods and this is why e-learning will be very convenient to help within organisations because it is constantly changing and this change would help employees improve on their learning and training and will be able to implement new skills within the workplace.

Why does HR needs e-learning in nowadays organization? Firstly before I go into detail about how e-learning helps HRD perform you will need to know what e-learning actually is. E-learning used to be known as computer-based learning, this is basically what it still is, it is a way of learning but on a computer or even these days there is even m-learning which is through the mobile. We need e-learning in everyday life to be able to adapt the required skills in education, employment, even at home. It can be defined as any learning activity supported by information and communication technologies which is known as ICTs. There are arguments out there concerning the labels, an example of this is whether ICT-based learning is the same as e-learning, we can gather information from the world wide web channel and this would be our online materials, but we can also get materials from this intranet would could be confused as being from the world wide web but instead this material is delivered through an internal network of personal computers. E-learning is in fact taken to mean any form of electronic technology which can support learning this can be opposed to the chalk and blackboard technology which used to be the main form of learning.

· Why is HR strategy important to influence nowadays organizational success?

In organizational level, humans do formalize strategies as a function to direct and focus their efforts. However, in a business organizational ( a firm), such efforts will focus on creating value for profit. In fact, the environment is a market with limited resources and therefore it causes competition exists. This environment mght be more or less stable, but it is in constant change.

HR Strategy will become a systemic and rational act, a process that can be managed in order to successfully attain in the golas of the firm. HR Strategy can divide these three kinds. Firstly, a HR plan is intended to achieve a particular purpose and to develop a HR strategy for dealing with unemployment. It is overall HR strategy to gain promotion. For government ( public organization's economic HR strategy example. Secondly, it is the process of HR planning or putting a HR plan into operation in a skillful way.

Finally, for war strategy, it is the skill of HR planning to be trained to the movements of armies in s battle or war. An example, of military HR training strategy, defend, strategies compare tactic.

However, nowadays, business organizations need " office of general", " command" , " generalship" skillful actions, leadership and leading welfare from one leader, such as CEO who have any effective HR strategy to manage staffs and tasks as well as leading them to serve their organizations successfully. So, an effective HR strategy can give good HR planning direction to let the organization to know whether it ought need how to do in order to achieve its HR development goals successfully.

An effective HR planning direction can achieve the organizaton's HR allocation goals more easily. For example, knowing how it can use of common resources ( e.g. available human and technological resources). A basic HR strategic advantage tool win and prevail over rivals in the market comes from the differentiated used of such resources.

How HRM strategy changes in beverage industry?

In beverage competitive industry example, Coca-Cola soft drink organization example, it was still keeping its predominance in the beverage market product " Coke", Pepsi Co was advancing fast on the base of a successful "image" HR strategy targeting the youngest segment of the beverage market under the taste of the new generation. So, it can select to employ more young workers to work in its organization in order to persuade many youngest soft drink customers to believe it is one young soft drink health drinking company. By 1983, Pepsi had begun to outsell coke in supermarkets when coke maintained its edge only through soda vending machines and fast food restaurants. Although, different marketing strategic breakthrough by far unexpected. It follows all time successful formula of coke. In 1985, the " New Coke" was introduced after an extensive study of market trended, surveys, focus group and taste tests strategies. In these survey investigation process, it must need to employ many part time or full time questionnaires staffs, they can include students, housewives, freelance workers, unemployed workers. So, HR department needs have enough time to select the right applicants to finish the whole questionnaire investigation project efficiently and effectively. The HR arrangement need to gather information to conclude this goals, such as how to design the new formula ( or taste) was based on a different ( lower cost) source of sugar, high fructose corn syrup to replace cane sugar. All of Coca ( the plant from which comes the allealoid cocain) derivates were also removed from the old formula. So, how to design the taste is the main survey information gathering aim. Also, how HR arrangement which can have enough questionnaire staffs to carry on gathering information from the taste tests in the limited time to achieve to finish the taste test questionnaire project efficiently and effectively.

What are HR strategic benefits? They include: It can assist an organization to protect its HR capital base. It is a well accepted business principle, it can also help the organization to extend this notion to the world' natural and human resources, it can help leaders to plan and measure HR employment and reward and welfare and performance management systems of business enterprises more accurately, it can help business leaders to do the best balance between narrow self-interest and actions takes for the good of unemployment or creating more opportunity solution benefit in society as well as they can do actions in pursuit of financial survival more easily.

Why can HR strategy help organizational change in success? Knowing the importance and implication of organizational change and admitting the fact that organizational change success and leader / leadership can play a key role in bringing and implementing these changes by deciding the desired form of an organization and taking the potential steps which are needed for the process. So, when one organization has one good HR strategy, it can assist its organization to change more people and non-people resources effectively and efficiently.

Why do organizations need to change HR strategy? Nowadays, dynamic business environments influence organizations that respond quickly and effectively to constant change. A dynamic enterprise has two important tasks. It must adapt the current business environment, e.g. people skillful shortage in the industry into a shared HR strategy and then quickly and effectively to employ talent people or potential people to do the skillful job for its organization.

Reference

Andy, W.C. and Barry, J. B. and Wai, M.M. (2002) , Managing human resource in Hong Kong, Hong Kong: Thomson, p.6

Black, J. A., & Boal, K. B. (1994). Strategic resources: Traits, Configurations and paths to sustainable competitive advantage. Strategic Management Journal, 15: 131-148.

Craig, E.A. & Stephen, L.M. & John, L.W. (2011) family business compensation: New York, US, Palgrave Macmillan, p.35

Driving change at general motor, 2005, online retrieved 15 Dec. 2009, www.cioleadershipnotes.com/p/gm/htm

General motor talking swift cost cutting action, 2008, online retrieved 15 Dec. 2009 from dailymarkets.com/stock/2008/11/24/General- motor-takingswift-cost-action-cutting.

Kumar, S. (2005) "IKEA's globalization strategies and its foray in China", IBS center for management research Stephen, R.B. Organizational development, U.S., The McGraw- Hill , 2011, pp.5-8

Source: The harvard model of HRM

Beer , M., specter, B., Lawrence, PR. and Mills, D. Q. (1984). managing human assets. New York: Free press.

John, B. & Jeff, G. ( 6 edition, 2017). Human resource management theory and practice, Palgrave, Macmillan publishers ltd. UK , London,pp.4-5

John, H. (2013) managment a very short introduction, Oxford university press, UK, pp.11-13

Leon, M. (2002). High performers, how the best companies find and keep them: US, Jossey - Bass, John Wiley & Sons, Inc, US pp.133-134

Robert P. V, (6 edition, 2006). organizational behavior: core concepts: US, Thomson, pp.58

Sources

http://info.shine.com/industry/automobiles-auto-ancillaries/2.html retrieved on 14 th May 2014

https://www.kpmg.de/docs/auto-survey.pdf retrieved on 17 the June 2014

Printed by Libri Plureos GmbH in Hamburg,
Germany